AF413542

INTERSTITIAL

Annie Lure

Table of Contents

DIONYSUS' MAIDEN

In this tableau, my grandmother's ankles
scab with grape cuticles; the internee's

hapless step rattles the cobblestones
as if orphaned cradles. How he seeks

succor in my grandmother's stucco
house: a block of nougat for his trussed tongue.

How the treed pomegranates put together their heads,
ancestors caucusing, and the internee

produces his unconsummated deed-
a hand missing a finger-

and my grandmother lifts her ruddy foot
like bounty out of the trough:

Pay me the remaining 300 LEK[1]
or I'll have your head like the grapes.

How the first cousin-once-removed
pincers the house like a boa

vowing to excise the internee
as if it were a house mouse

----

[1] 1 Albanian currency

so that my grandmother can then impute
the house to the cousin's name.

How the internee returns to the house
as if a darkling son to his surrogate mother.

How the cousin leans like a scepter
against the stucco wall he makes a throne.

And my grandmother is widowed twice over:
a hierodule sans temple.

She stomp-stomp-stomps the grapes
to reconstitute her husband.

GIFTS

(Ekphrasis)

Artwork: Prolonged and Undiminished Applause
Artist: Aleksei Sundukov

The masses proffer their brains as if wreaths to Stalin.

Stalin hoards their brains the way a schoolboy hoards candy.

Poor Stalin's got no face. The sun burned it off. The rain washed it out.
A hoarded brain munched it.

His devotees peel their faces and paste them where his should be.

Stalin sieves smiles onto the masses like an industrious mother.

But the brainy few eschew the smiles. Pray tell, dear leader, isn't your
'production mode' a capitalist investment?

Stalin gazes at his gilded mirror the way Yahweh gazed at the face of
the antediluvian Earth: Let there be no thinking man.

Stalin whisks the brains with a flick of his finger. But some brains
adhere to their skulls.

Stalin lobotomizes the brains. The palms sew their lifelines into his
placard sticks.

Dear citizens, we have converted the counterrevolutionaries.

The masses strike their hands, flint with steel, igniting a prolonged and undiminished applause.

The artist labors underground, high on turpentine. His brush incantates his hand. It wards off Stalin's commissions for an idol and an idyll.

The confiscated brains of his countrymen ring the bell of his head. He limns a box about his effaced, brainless people.

His painting rides his vigor. It blooms on the wall of Zimmerli Art Museum.

The bloody applause clangs my brain.

THE DEAD BOY'S RELATIVES'
HAMARTIA

The paternal grandmother lathers
cortisone on the flaking child, *may you*
become robust, my heart, palmful
after palmful, she scorns the doctor's
frugality (didn't he say only a smidgen a day?),
weaving unbeknownst to her
Nessus[2] chiton. The boy's feverish skin
is now his funeral pyre[3]. Bad blood
murders the air between the doctor
and the boy's mother:
'*You killed your own child* snaps like manacles around the mother's
hands.
'*Half of me had to tend my* own *dying mother*!'
is broken up like a genotype.

The young mother gravid with guilt
wombs the blighted boy
in her palms as if to rebirth him.

The maternal grandmother is charged posthumously,

---

[2] Greek myth of Nessus' tunic: Imbued with venom, Nessus' tunic inflicts
unbearable pain on its wearer.
[3] Unable to bear the pain, Heracles, Nessus' tunic's hapless recipient, prepares a
funeral pyre.

interpellated as Heracles'[4] anima:[5]
her haste into death consigned the boy
to a careworn, benighted Deianeira[6].

The pathway to the mourning house is strewn
with cobblestones like blasted brains.
The visiting cousin vacates the boy's father's
lap of the serving tray as if vacuuming a miserly uterus.

The coffee cup is clogged like a coronary
with the paternal grandmother's grief.
Between cup and saucer we graft
paper blessings to freshen her humor.

[4] Watching the centaur Nessus carry his wife, Deianeira, across the river and force
himself upon her, Heracles shoots an arrow tinged with poison at him.
[5] Greek mythology/Jungian psychology: the feminine aspect of a man's personality
[6] Deianeira, foolishly believing the fatally wounded Nessus' telling her that his
blood would ensure Heracles' fidelity, takes his stained tunic to Heracles.

DELEUZE'S WITCH'S LINE

Red lights. The TV casts off its cape. CNN presides as oracle. A Honduran caravan pries open America's thighs. Calls to wall off America. Give her a chastity belt.

Let me strum my pubic hairs as if they were the strings of my childhood *çifteli*[7]. On the Rutgers quad. Inside the Met. Before the White House.

My people, the British say, are white people dining cross-legged on the floor like Indians.

Half of my face is a poorly carved early Sumerian statue; the other half, an ironing of bleached blond hair like a doughnut dunked in latte.

Shkodër, Albania: Fog hangs over the Buna river like a presentiment. Three brothers labor stone into a castle. Each midnight tolls the castle's fall, requiring their rebuilding. Immure one of your wives, a mendicant old man advised them. Whomever serves you lunch the next day. But don't make her privy to it.

I was immured in a psychiatric facility. But my tongue flew out like a peregrine.

The Hondurans are real. The caravan is not.

---

[7] A long-necked, two-stringed mandolin

I love an Iraqi whose flesh tastes of Basra dates and whose words gush like the Euphrates.

I am the offspring of a cyborg and a subhuman.

My mother pours sigmas, deltas, and Maxwell's equations into my breakfast bowl. She earned her sparking green eyes in faraway conferences and set them as if globes on her desk of a face.

My father hobbles like a three-legged dog from bank cash handling to supermarket stocking. Albania tugs at him like a spurned mistress. His maladroitness hounds me into car wreckage.

Rosafa[8], the wife of the youngest brother, was sacrificed on the altar of honesty; but, she had one last request: Immure me with my right eye exposed, my right hand exposed, and my right breast exposed so I may tend my son. The castle surges forth milk.

Oh, Baby! The blond man tosses the word like a used-up condom.

Enunciate, little boy! I have heisted your lexis. I erected my English-English dictionary as a tent in the parking lot at Fairfield Apartments, Newark, Delaware. I lit up my pen as a cigarette and pawed for words. 'Exogenous', I flared. I tucked 'cynosure' into the fold of my brain as if a gala invitation. I smoked out 'bowdlerize'.

---

[8] Cf.: Legend of Rosafa

I have immured myself on the topmost floor of Alexander Library. I open Arshi Pipa's[9] tome to disinter my mother. A monstera pats my shoulder with its many-pronged hand like a dissembling mother-in-law.

You cannot rape me, blond boy. Rape is for women with a sanctity to preserve. I'll just reclaim the Albanian figs I gifted you. Or else I'll snap your neck as if it were a chastity belt:

For I have eaten women's libidos as if they were juicy steaks. For I have forked men's brains into my maw.
I am supra-sexual. A sphinx. Mohammad Ali Pasha's daughter[10].

---

[9] 9Albanian linguist and poet
[10] Albanian ruler of Ottoman Egypt

A LEVELING OF PREFERENCES

I saunter past the topiary bears,
my hypothalamus ironed like a pair of Cameroonian breasts,
the clinics ahead a strand of implanted teeth.

Good morning, Ms.
Perhaps this will be more tolerable — slow-release Progestin!
I just need to make an incision
on your arm. In some medieval church,
amid wickedly smelling wicks,
the heretic's fork smiles
into the flesh of some jacana woman.

On the way back, a spraying of luteal petals.
They've the color of Miss Havisham's dress.
My soul is spayed is what I write.

My eggs are cut off from circulation,
stored in an empress' bedchamber.
or else conveyed into Anna Swir's minus life poem.
The drums tighten their hyena clitoris skins.
The men with faces scooped like Snow White cakes
not the ones dripping testosterone from the stage sets
of their cheekbones light up my nucleus accumbens.
I am pilloried in contraceptive scent. My sweaty Budweiser
flaps like the manicured hand of an absconding woman.
The bar's tabletop is de-realized as trapdoor. I see Anise.
Aniseed bathing in thermal waters amid minty crags,
a bundle of sexy son genes on her shoulder.

Genes she smuggled some hot night.

I stab my nun-black pen:
My ovary is a spinster
dozing under the tarry roof
of some Third World asylum is what I write.

PORTRAIT: POMEGRANATES

My grandmother's pomegranates glow on tabletops, swell on windowsills, and rub each other in baskets. *Grandma, what is beyond the pomegranate orchard?* My grandmother scatters the arils on a clay dish. *A fearsome dragon lives there.* My thighs burn. I wonder who my husband will be. *Don't venture there.* There was once a girl who strapped on her iron shoes and trekked the mountain. She smelled like pomegranates to the resident dragon. The protagonist of a recreational novel told the man with the paintbrush arms: Let me be your escort, your screw-sheeted nude. *Don't venture there.* The dragon ordered the girl to cry into a cauldron so as to drink her tears upon returning from his hunt. She tricked him with salt. I am overcome with dragon lust, but my grandmother wants to ensconce me inside a pomegranate. The second night, the dragon ordered the girl to partake of human flesh, but she fed it to the horse. When the dragon returned from his hunt, he called out to the flesh: Flesh, where are you? I am here, ensconced in the warm belly. My grandmother lies on a leaden hospital bed. Tendrils of spit stream out like galaxies from the universe of her mouth. She is drunk with a shot of God. *They will remove you, granddaughter, flesh of my flesh, from me. They will seduce you with chocolate-pomegranate torte.* In the Colosseum, Alypius foisted the bloodlust of the gladiatorial games upon the masses. *Grandma, I manned the dragon!* The dragon surrendered to the girl's cleverness and led her to his bedroom. In the recreational novel, the protagonist told her man: I will bury you in a graveyard of easels. *It will be too late, granddaughter.* The dragon told the girl to undress. She told him that for each petticoat she removes, he must shed a layer of hide. He stripped into a handsome man. *Who are 'they', grandmother? Here, have two pomegranates from my husband, the dragon!* Behind my grandmother's glaucous eyes, a girl shirks the sea's wheedling.

NINEVEH: A LAMASSU'S CONFESSIONS

Men with steak hair   trowel hands   mattock feet evicted me
from Nineveh's womb   they broke up the binding of dirt
I had guarded
the empires of Tiglath-Pileser Ashurbanipal   Sennacherib
until Christianity's takeover   and Islam's takeover demoted me to
dust   Ashur's sentinel neutered
Nineveh encrypted my gypsum with the fingerprints of Ashur's builders
and votaries
These foreigners kidnapped me   They said they were excavators
I bled Assyrian poppics from Nineveh to London
They trafficked me to Adam Lowe[11]   He said he was an   art
historian
and brandished a white-light scanner   his teammates
brandished theirs
as if responding to a war cry   they mounted them on tripods
soldiers behind parapets shooting spectrally broadband illumination at
my cleft
Lecherous light striated my body   the psychiatrist's medico-sexual
regime *Did you yield to the Medes' penetration?*
I excreted a cloud of a million data

---

[11] The names, as well as some of the practices, in this poem are recapitulated from
Michael Dumiak's 'Ancient Sculptures Return to Mosul as Digitally
Reconstructed Replicas', which appeared on IEEE Spectrum on February 23,
2018.

We are your protectors, dear. The British Museum values your
intactness. Now, tell us, where may we find the other Lamassu?
Faceless   effaced men decapitate my brethren
Their scimitars slice with the colonizers' frisson   Lucas Petit
like Balzac's duenna lassoes my neck
He feeds me technicolor hay in the marquee: *The Horse with the*
Golden Eyes
Ashur's sentinel Disney-fied
They carve my likeliness from a polyurethane monolith
          Mother Nineveh
I languish in their pavilion   my body cancered with their rays
They will graft me to their imperial museum
My gypsum must gleam with paeans to my appropriators'
resourcefulness
I must smirk at my inheritors' recognizing gasps
But I will roar like Ashur   Mother Nineveh
Ashur's sculptors will replenish your sons
and you will bar the simulacrum from entering you
You will curse him as the colonizers' mocked up mockery of a son You
will set the Tigris against him   Mother Nineveh

PORTRAIT OF WOMAN IN RESIDENTIAL FACILITY

Woman, sipping whole milk, his sperm
clotting your eyelashes, you swear upon

the cicatrix cross of your impromptu tattoo
and straitjacket gift bow. Woman, wrapped

in a cheesecloth of frost,
treading naked in the garden,

you gather dandelions and the stares
of children sticking like needles

on the arms of balconies. Woman, their eyes
appear silvery in morning's sun, and your urine

drips the last Naiad. Woman, you cast your chalice
of an eye upon the swarthy girl. You want

to snatch her away, comb her haphazard
hair, and lay her to sleep with a butterfly

kiss on her forehead. Woman
with a body tinier than your heart.

THE RUNNER, AVON BEACH

A woman collared with the sea, seagulls for earrings,
her two dogs corralled scourges the shore,
her muscles cudgeling the spindrift of her footfalls
She's a diurnal Hecate.
Overhead, a helicopter whirrs away like an exposed culprit.
Dyed with the maccha green of the weekly garden club,
I circumambulate the boardwalk bench.
A couple allofeeds each other its love story.
The woman pounds the seashore, her muscles dark with dolphin lust.
The spume is a desecrated wedding veil.
A child sprawling a red blanket
collapses into the sand of nonbirth.
My ice-cream self-cannibalizes in the 10 A.M. sun.
The seagulls lance the beach with their cries.
The beach retches its shells.
The woman and her dogs ripple like filigreed umbilici.
I lurk behind the bench how an estranged daughter lurks
out of the frame of a family photograph.
I cock my fingers around the woman
and fix her scene with afterbirth.

DEAR NATIVE LANGUAGE

"… insular thinking that favors language preservation over language growth"
—Jennifer Manoukian, *Language and Globalization*, Edited by Maryam Borjian

My language, we lap your blood
and grow sanguine with tales
of our brows arching like bud-
enlaced iron over the enemy's pocking
our hills with our heads.

But you whiten into alabaster statue:
your tongue hung on the kitchen hook
your breasts decanted and clacked as sacraments
your sex thumbed in community gatherings.
You starch into a pall stretching for generations.

My language, your blood
alchemizes our innards to gold.
The slain cannot slay, we say,
only halo themselves
to burn off lambasting lips,
everlastingly resplendent.

My language, I want to vitiate you,
lick in the solecisms of my hybrid tongue.
I want to induce birth pains
so that you may deliver us

from the alps to engineering laboratories,
that you may run amok across continents,
that we may bloom forth like infant pudenda.

Love,   23
Your New Speaker

OFFENSIVE THINGS

To most: A swastika spidering the bartender's shaved scalp.

To some: A penis nudging a cross.

To the self-anointed elite: The dog ceased serving it's (its) master.

Expected to all: A white schoolboy paints on a tile in fluorescent green and halcyon yellow a black schoolboy dangling from a tree.[12]

Expected to all: A man spoons caviar against the backdrop of a dust-bitten child begging on the scrawny street.[13]

Expected to none: Nurse proffers you a saccharine smile with *happy pills* as you await a bed in a facile feelgood facility.

Expected to none: An NGO worker clinks in front of a displaced family two prosthetic legs as if toasting their son while B-2s drop bombs like bubble bath balls.

To dissident feminists/women lancing their sisters (read: the disabused): The TV gapes vagina- like on the living room wall: *He raped me twenty years ago. I was twenty. He serves in the senate, but in fact he is a miscreant who…*

---

[12] *Blacked Out*. A film by the Highland Park African American History Project. Highland Park, a self-congratulatory town, confronts its deep-seated racism and de facto segregation. Directed by John Hulme.
[13] *The Five Obstructions*. A joint documentary by Jorgen Leth and Lars von Trier, which explores the construct of the 'perfect human'.

To virile men who feel emasculated/superfluous: A woman hawking 'Hands Off My Vagina' lube tubes.

To me: An obscenely large Listerine bottle flashing its chemo amber on the shelf of Walgreens.

GHAZAL: NON-WOMAN

Sans pudenda, hysterectomy-ed, I am a non-woman.
Shorn of breasts, in self-imposed askesis, I am a non-woman.

Transgendered through assiduousness for her wife Ianthe,
Iphis accedes to her father Ligdus' ideal: a non-woman.

I grind against my own brain, an intellectual-in-training
encircled by the power circuit I interrogate: a non-woman.

In *A Straight Mind*, Monique Wittig enjoins lesbians
to smash the bigendered copula: a lesbian is a non-woman.

The precious tone-on-tone blue baby doll frock
desexualizes the pregnant woman: a dolled up non-woman.

On Jean Genet's stage, the light flowers a beard
on the smooth chin of a man playing a woman: a non-woman.

With your pen, Annie, you lance Rebecca Solnit's *Men Explain
Things to Me*: Subsuming the 'other' women under one's privilege
blanches them non-women.

I WAS ASSIGNED TO WRITE A DOCUMENTARY

Welcome to Highland Park, New Jersey. The children beat pumpkins to a pulp.

Rachel Dolezal doffs her whiteness
at Boho Exotic Studio: *Coif me a black body.*
Black hair is a fine specimen. Pin it!
My weave is my lectern. Who heard the minstrel bird sing?

Dr. Ben Carson: I am black as a brain-encrusted sole / my hand was made for swinging a mother- slicing machete / but through the white light of God I twirl brain retractors.

The boy is black as obsidian.
He is cossetted in his family,
which is cossetted in academia.
And the neighbor is white as hemlock.
The boy is in fact nestled among many such hemlocks.
The boy clicks out a photo of the neighbor's house
as if popping a bubblegum.
The neighbor calls the police.
Six police cars blare the road.
And the boy run-run-rides the fugitive's wind.
And the ghosts of Tamir Rice Treyvon Martin Michael Brown Freddie Gray whoosh through him.

HOMEGROWN

The bar is called Homegrown.
Its men are homegrown
on Evil Genius® and Party Crasher®.
Est-ce que tu parles français?
The man in Barbour jacket
hypostatizes Provencal glasses
in my printed scarf.
No, I'm not French. I toss
my car keys like contraband
on the table. He reads Camille Paglia,
that academic siren, he tells me.
Civilization is contiguous to savagery.
His hand twirls like a prima ballerina.
The frat boy's prehensile fingers
vis-à-vis the cleavage recall the hunter
arrowing an elephant. Two tables to our right, a gazelle
grazes on Vegemite®. *The toothed vagina,* I quote
is no sexist hallucination. And she's right.
The upside-down glasses on the bar rack
clink like succubae over the men's heads.
Every man is lessened post-coitally inside every woman.
The gaze of the acrylic woman on the wall,
like a Papin sister, bludgeons his heart.
We are not afraid of women. His mouth is
Anne Sexton's car fuming carbon monoxide.
I can drug you. I flaunt my mouth like a magician's
unbreakable glass. *And then slice you up.*
Sure, you can do anything, he eyes the capped tooth ashtray.
But men are not a priori afraid of women's overpowering them.

"Meat is Murder" by The Smiths cleaves the air.
The table de-realizes as citadel.
I circumambulate it atavistically like a groundskeeper.
The light from the fixture butcher-papers his face.
I sharpen my finger on his pulse:
Do you want to know where I am from?
and grab his dick as if it were minced meat.
My breath palls his lips like the roses
my grandmother thieved when I was eight
from our neighbor's garden so she could syrup them for me.

SUICIDE DRESS

girl in *tear* dress or *suicide* dress
painting with nail polish
or lipstick or blush splotches
of vulvas or apples or botched hearts
girl slicing the pulp of fiction
curlicues of poems snaking
up her stocking earrings
hang themselves on her earlobes
a necklace crucifies itself
on her breast that crackle-
painted leather jacket is a cast
for a fashionably broken
torso or arm and the erect fir cones
how they scream of her flesh

SLEEPING BEAUTY

sleeping beauty how you sleep
in this dirty street scrawny street-
lamps slice your white
apple of a heart with their sick
sick glow the gutter gulps
your pearly earring who snicked
it off your ear you little beauty
the glittery prince who shakes
fairy dust out of his hair
the boy with filigree
on his knee ah princess you
pricey princess with your swan-
white chiffon dresses doting
on your dove-y/dove-y breasts princess
sealing kisses in ivory boxes
primped for a prick of a prince
who pricks your lacey vein
with his morphine lips
and whips the white
of your throat with that billowing
black of his and clack-clack-
clacks away that prick
and night drip-drip-drips
and sleep breaks its limbs
and jagged rocks rock-rock-rock you

AGARWOOD

In inimical land, wearing her bra like bandolier, Sana prowls the taverns. She spiderwebs men's minds and limbs: *my nipples are sweet agar. I am at your service.* But the agar scums in these men's mouths. They imbibe the curses of Sana's beloved Imi-Gur. Enervated, they fall onto Sana's bed the way Imi-Gur's crenelated towers fell to them and their brethren. Sana splays their bodies on her altar and cuts them up. They shed carnelian as if from Imi-Gur's marrow. *Oh, son of Imi-Gur! The earth grinds your heart. Oh, daughter of Imi-Gur! The earth sips your soul. I am still alive.*

Fallen is Imi-Gur the great. Its children's entrails ribbon its hills. Its valleys rock grandmothers' lullabies and fathers' exhortations. No bread is braided in its markets. No thighs are braided in its bedrooms. The encroachers carried sheaves of women out of Imi-Gur. Sana heard the mountains shriek as she was led away. She saw figs hang themselves on the fig trees, denying the invaders their velvety sweetness. She passed the houses of her precinct, their occupants excised from them, their doorsteps retching under the effluvium. Sana's memory held all: her mother's manuscripts, inked with curlicues like Imi-Gur's rivers, her sister's hair azalea-ing forth, and the incarnadine words the flames of her hearth spoke to her and her lover. Her slain lover's 24-karat blood kindled her veins. Sana's chest hardened like Imi-Gur's wood. Revenge infected her heart, curdling in her breasts and oozing like agar out of her nipples.

In inimical land, she manacles her eyelids with mascara. She inhabits a half-finished brick house. She sheltered herself in this house after she evaded her captors. It is not so much a house as a former anvil workshop where men hammer out their unruly hearts. With quilts, she set up an altar. She makes art of the men's bodies she seizes. It recalls her washing sheets by Imi-Gur's river and spreading them out on rocks or her fingers working traceries on her lover's body. She haunts an inimical land for men. This land of locusts and anvils gormandizes on Imi-Gur's treasures. Its markets pat their bellies. The land clothes its women with Imi-Gur's ramie. It feeds its children out of Imi-Gur's celadon bowls. It bedecks its dwellings with the lapis lazuli its men abducted from Imi-Gur. These men plundered fertile Imi-Gur to spare themselves internecine warfare because the land that reared them is as desolate as their hearts. The meagerness of the grain turns these men's fingers into sabers.

"My nipples are sweet agar. I serve you," Sana shrouds the man's eyes with her breath. Smoke, like a haze of bees, wafts about the tavern. But the man's eyelids, sharp as falcon talons, tear through the film. His hand steels into a saber. The wine roils like blackened blood in its cask. The man plunges the blade into Sana's heart. Her breast bursts into litanies of song. Fallen is Imi- Gur the great. Its avenger, too, is fallen.

Her flesh is pleated into belles-lettres. She is postcard-ized and sold in the markets of an inimical land.

I WANT HER

I want her. She's that sprayed-with-perfume letter
I didn't write & she's the lacy panties
I strung around someone's arm
& she's got the libido
I'd like to chew how I chew gum
& oh how she grooms the wind
w/ manicured-in-pitch-red fingers! I want her nipple:
suck-suckle-suck-suckle
silk & milk & silk & milk
nip-nibble-nip-nibble
cherries-berries-cherries-berries.
I want the L-s of her labia.
I want her pony her peony all her lucky charms
& all the men she rides on wet nights
& all the pearls she pries from mouths.
I want to lick her lipstick shtick.

A FEMALE THING

She's a rack of lush/blush womanish knacks:
a fine jeweled spine
mined from too many men-caves,
a tongue she coils into a red-hot rose,
a lusty liver to break down men-bits.
She's opium, an opening
of geranium petals,
her hair incense sticks,
her sex a bed of coals, a bowl of strawberries
she spoons to men-mouths,
a piano tune, desire's notes & syllables — LI-BI-DO, LI-BI-DO.

NUTRITIONAL PARIAH

The debris-clogged gutters disgorge the rain ramming into them. You sit cross-legged, naked, and eldritch in the blue light that the TV screen licks onto the carpet. You chew your son's transdermal patch. A psychiatrist prescribes it to him for an attention deficit disorder. In his classes, he blows balloons, which he punctures with the nib of his pen when he should be writing. Spasms circumambulate your flesh. You squint at Loretta. She is glassed and chewing on air. She chews on her mother's text: *it is time.* Her mother, the voiceover swells, has coerced her to participate in her stepfather's murder. The mother's husband is impotent fruit that the mother abrogates. *A nutritional pariah*, I think. The mother has deemed his one-million-dollar life insurance benefits more enriching than his flesh or his words or his furniture-repairing prowess. Loretta chokes on her mother's *I love you.* You want to resuscitate her. You crawl toward the TV and fit your lips into her bluish ones. The fake palm tree implanted in the peaty soil of our pot convulses in its want to draw nutrients. You bang you fist against the screen as the muscles of your back rise like pegs. I steady your shoulder and cup my hands in front of your mouth. You spit out the filmy patch as if expelling some diseased organ. I wrap a blanket around you, unburden your eye of locks of hair, and brew you some chrysanthemum tea.

You left Jody for me, even though the two of you had great sex, even though her juices would overflow, now saccharine, now tangy. I am strictured as a varnished table. I was un-orgasmic until you dialed my nipples. Jody has no brain, you tell me. But I am *palliating.* I absorb something of the teapot. You like the way I tend you. And your son likes me. He and I versify whenever we meet. I write out '*we splash about the fountain*' and underneath it '*tomorrow I'll climb the* _____*tain'*. He fills in the blank with an M squiggly as a balloon neck, and our words bubble forth.

"Gina left her son in the car." You rest your head like a disenchanted prince on the pillow.

"What?" I leaf through the slim volume of Erich Auerbach's *Mimesis.* He posits that writing is superfluous. The telos of realistic representation is no literature at all.

"She got out and ran up to meet her dealer. She told me to go with her. Her son was in the car. She just forgot about him and never came back that night."

"What did you do? Where is he now?"

The rain pours its patter into your mouth.

The fridge groans like a hungry child's stomach. I open it as if parting your thighs. It is barren save for half a Granny Smith apple and a smidgen of vanilla and peanut butter ice cream. The fridge is barren like a hysterectomy-d woman. I take out the cup of ice cream and kiss it. I dig a diaphanous red spoon into the vestal body of the cream and lift it laden to my lips. I hold the cream in my mouth longer than is necessary. I practice that which is not nourishing. I consecrate the cream in the altar of my tongue.

GARTH GREENWELL READING, RUTGERS, NEW BRUNSWICK

Garth Greenwell writes dirty prose
dirty as Anacreon's Thracian filly, amongst bat-naked Bulgarians,
those bastardized Greeks. *Where is Bulgaria?* The American mind is
clotted like noncirculating wealth. Garth's reed pipe voice
disports the querying woman, and I smirk, a cynosure of my own
seafaring.
Bulgaria is spraddled in eastern Europe   one thigh bridled by
Russia   the other discharged
like premature ejaculate into the orifices of the European Union.
I was a double exile. Garth
in his hierophant's coat as if in a film noir,
face and hands like a closeted Galatea,
descending from the ivoried Palace of Culture
into some sublunary realm, Sofia's lip-printed bathrooms,
an illiterately sheened body signaling its intention to suck.
This must have been Colette's den, or else the backwaters
of my apartment in Tirana
in which the baker's piping burst like a drunken brawl,
and my neighbor Valentina scorned her son's soft speech:
You are not gay. Americanized gays talk like houseflies trapped in ewers.
Are there gay communities in Bulgaria?
(Two penises overhanging CNN town halls on homophobia.)
Bulgarians talk of the Turks' penetration and the communists'
surveillance implants and whatever somatic circuits the Orthodox
Church buzzes.
Writing programs fanned out like iambs on Garth's computer screen in
Kentucky.

Garth eschewing the écorché of a sentence:
To write muscular prose is to acquiesce to the straight body.
I wanted to be a large promiscuous queer body
to spin legs like bottles with those wine-shaded Bulgarians
and muddy up on the banks of the Danube sentences
about the Romanians calling the Bulgarians, their immediate
neighbors, thieves. The heads of the Rutgers auditorium sway in the
meniscus of Garth's wine voice but mine is the only one that leaps up:
The Starova family
in my native Albania, I write, traces its roots to Bulgaria,
and by day I would interrogate endocentric expressions with their son
but by night the Aromanian boy from across the street and I
would fall into the spell of a story, tickle that story's scrotum as well as
its G-spot.

THE ELDERLY EMIGRES

The elderly Albanian woman accepted her second cousin's basement
in New York with the curtsy of a much-maligned hostess.

She arranges bell peppers like dentures on the countertop,
then sidles outside to pet the brownstone wall.

Fanning her eyelashes like a pair of male birds of paradise,
she snaps a selfie: I love my friends back home!

Her husband, the eminent mathematician, pendulates
like Peter between aisled rows of Campbell Soup cans.

The communist regime scourged his youth with his bad biography.[14]
Its henchmen took his villa as if landfilling roadside dog shit.

An icon zipped in scarecrow clothes, he trudges his cart
toward the trope of promised land. Car exhausts furl his face like perdition.

His wife tore her knee ligaments weeks ago the way family ties are cut.
He gives her the teat of Coffee Mate to milk a few drops of manna

and sits by the table, hanging his head sideways. What he cannot
teach in English tumors inside his bunker-black larynx.

Her prune flesh coruscates in the Facebook limelight:
Long day. Finally done. Me in front of our beautiful house.

---

[14] Phrase designates an Albanian citizen-subject's having engaged in activities
considered inimical to the then communist regime.

The replies scatter like second wedding petals:
Oh, Xhuli, you're so lucky! You bought that house fast!

The drapes flapping her face make a hellish boudoir
and when she puckers her lips, it is Clotho's[15] bloody thread:

Yes, I did, while you all breathe inside one-bedroom apartments
parceled out by the former regime like cudgels of bread.

____

[15] The youngest sister of the three Fates in the Greek pantheon, she spins the
threads of life.

THE CRIER'S GRANDDAUGHTER

My grandmother is hunched like a gnarled index finger over the funeral scene. Her tears oil the spanakopita earth: *May our kisses embalm you, oh dear one.* The sun flagellates her back. The wind pecks her flesh.

Forgive me, grandmother. I have sacralized you.

Rewrite: The town's mayor is my grandmother's thirty-ninth client for this month.

Forgive me, grandmother. I have whored you out.

A roll of brocade on the sewing table. Beside it, wolf muzzle flowers. The pirated cassette tapes roll like innards. Grandmother's shrillness insinuates a murder of crows embroidering carrions.

How morbid! Cousin Rudi cuts through the tableau. More a parody of morbidity. Rudi cannot sleep. The poesy of grief pulls her like Little Red Riding Hood's string. I roll a doxa into a joint. Here, Rudi. A regime of paroxysms.

The recording rolls on: *Se ke ikur qe femijje / i perfolur si qime ndonese ishe tra / O kurbet, kurbet i zi.*

I don my translator's turncoat. The mayor was slandered as hair though he was roof beam. A calque of the Albanian proverb carried on a caique to America. The sea was displayed black. I built an animal pen in my newfound home: a roomful of Roman genii. The editors deemed me a fraudulent American. They lopped off my telling in turn my grandmother's elegy.

I laminate myself with my pen: *Drinking a fifth of Jameson / I cannot spy the log in my own eye.*

Rouged like a captive woman turning into seductress, I find a roomful of batty houseflies.

My crier's lineage throttles its ersatz counterpart. Grandma, grandma they have slaughtered my genii.

SESTINA: INTERCESSOR

Costello bikes the highway in search of Eldorado.
He wants to escape an accountant's aridity
but happens upon the wasteland of Terlingua.
Inside a straw bale house, he meets a sage,
who advises him to bleed musical notes.
The ghosts gather about a campfire.

The ex-ghosts sputter stories in the campfire.
They extol the errant seeker of Eldorado,
how he knifed his body with musical notes
to replenish to leaf this land's aridity.
Counteract the witch's hex, said the sage,
and reclaim the civilization of Terlingua.

Costello learned the once abundant and proud Terlingua
grew arrogant so the witches stamped it out like a campfire.
To reaggregate it, you must sacrifice yourself, said the sage.
Costello felt like God. He could construct his own Eldorado.
The citizens' ghosted bodies flagellate and curse the aridity.
Costello scales the piano. Bandages of flesh stick with his notes.

Costello's blood whirls the once-ghosts as they sing his notes.
Mudbrick buildings sprout from the cracked earth of Terlingua.
A lithe river intercourses with it, tangoing away its aridity.
Revived trees oblate a kindling for the celebratory campfire.
With its homes coruscating in the sun, Terlingua is an Eldorado.
Stenciled, scrawled, guitar-picked is the abode of the sage.

I have a contract with the overlords of the land, says the sage,

to spot this fallen empire's intercessor and appeal to his notes.
He would be a romanticist, pursuing phantasmagoric Eldorado.
He would cradle and strum the body of our beloved Terlingua,
serenade its witch-inflicted pits as if rousing a campfire,
rub his head between the thighs of its aridity

and moisten the lips of this aridity.
He would recognize the hobo as a sage.
The hobo's tale would spark in him a campfire.
From his own flesh he would pluck notes.
His mouth would intone fruit in Terlingua.
He would embody the wealth of Eldorado.

The musician pours into the land's aridity notes.
 The sage nestles inside the bowels of Terlingua.
The citizens circumambulate their savior as if a campfire in Eldorado.

HOW TO BE A POEM

The poem ought to expurgate clichés with a militant's zeal. If the poem is to contain clichés, it ought to parade them like a Hallmark card fingering itself.

Convert 'there are ducks on the pond' into 'an imprinting of mallards cicatrices the pond'.

To birth a citadel, it behooves the poem to penetrate Damascus.

The poem must stand in front of the firing line and ruby its wounds.

The poem must vivify its predecessors with the prince's kiss.

The poem ought to show its face and then conceal it as if a phantom bride. A homely poem must have its oubliette.

A poem ought to collect images like spoons of rice in Buddha's begging bowl.

A poem ought to rattle you as if you were a baby's rattle.

WILL I CONSUMMATE MY WRITING?

(Tarot Poem)

The desert labors like a postmenstrual woman.
Its gatekeeper ties his bandana into a nuchal cord.
I stroke a phallus as if a comb. It pulses with a poem.
I peek through the thicket of phalli.
The sky licks itself like a contented cat.
I split the pod of a phallus.
It ejaculates a poem in the shape of a baby foot stump.

I Ghengis Khan[16] my animus.
I serry Assyrian warriors, Stalin, and the Me-Too women.
My fingers gobble my grandmother's pomegranate orchard.
I pottery wheel a pomegranate into a womb-well.
In it, I fish for folktales, which I then hook onto personae.
I fire pentacles of poems:
Nineveh encrypted my gypsum.
Stalin hoards their brains the way a schoolboy hoards candy.
The TV gapes vagina-like on the living room wall.
My writing hand is attached to a phallus strongarm.
Genial light helmets my head. My blood armors my body.
Critics lance my poem-heads.
I birth my agonism as poetry.
I oblate it in the corpus of a nubile woman.

The queen sits on a throne legged in phalli.

---

[16] Mongol warlord and emperor of largest contiguous empire

Two buffalo-black cats flank her like Do Kamissa's[17] doublets.
She wields a phallus as if Lachesis'[18] measuring rod.
She fans herself with my animus:
There was once an anemic girl, she recounts.
Amid the milk crusts of her room,
she penned stylized poems
of ribs rocking airy children
and indigents quaking on the eye's shore.
Echo[19] called out to Echo ad nauseum.
Then she read in IEEE Spectrum *of a Lamassu's expropriation.*
In it, she recognized her own displacement.
So, she lent her voice to the Lamassu.

The Lamassu's mourning mourned her mourning.
A mouth emptied itself into a navel ad nauseum.
A navel emptied itself into a mouth ad nauseum.
The girl visited Zimmerli Art Museum
and interpenetrated with a Russian nonconformist painting.
She severed all these exchanges from their *present times*
and overlaid them onto her *present time.*
The Lamassu brushed its woes onto Stalin's brainless masses.
A reader corresponded them to a kidnapped friend.
Thus, a coterie of itinerants grew into a settled tribe,

---

[17] Epic of Sunjata from the Malian Empire: Do Kamissa transmogrifies into a buffalo to ravage her brother Diarra's land for his ungratefulness.

[18] The middle sister of the Three Fates in the Greek pantheon, she measures the length of each life and appoints lots.

[19] Ovid's *Metamorphoses*: Echo and Narcissus. Hera, Zeus' wife, curses Echo, Zeus' adulteress, who protects his licentiousness, with speaking only by repeating the last few words of another's utterance.

which grew into a town, which grew into
a state, which grew into an empire.
Priapic,[20] the queen tips her penis, a scroll of poems, into a set of
scales.
My poems counterbalance a pile of gold.

The answer is hastened maturation perishes.

---

[20] Ithyphallic Roman god of fertility. Fresco of House of Vettii in Pompei shows
Priapus weighing his penis on scales counterbalanced with gold. A basket of fruit
flanks his feet. Possibly apotropaic.